MW01644369

Published by Latasha Nicole

ISBN 9798630374349

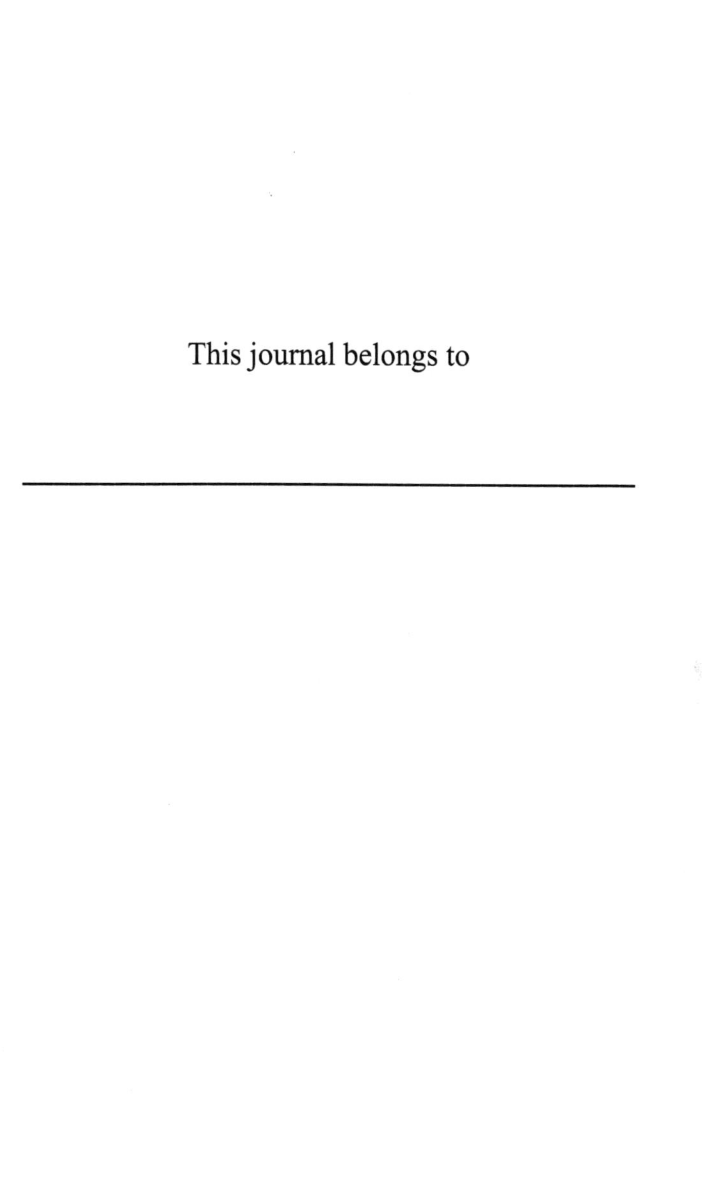

This journal belongs to

____

This journal is dedicated to every woman who has ever wished she could change the depth of her love for others in an effort to avoid betrayal, disappointment, and heartache.

As you embark on your journey to healing and truth through this journal, remember that the goal is not to learn how to love others less.
It's about establishing principles that help you heal and bounce back from offense while embracing the good, the bad, and the ugly embedded in your heart.

Each chapter provides a notes section for you to write down your thoughts and feelings on what is conveyed to you daily. I encourage you to be honest and be truthful, raw even, to find the freedom you so deserve.

Table of Contents

Day 31

♥

Psalms 51:10 - Create in me a clean heart, O God;

Dis-ease is simply the absence of ease, the absence of peace, and when something unclean comes in contact with broken skin, the wound becomes a breeding ground for infection. Likewise, there are people in your life who touched your heart with dirty hands. Whether you saw the signs of filth ahead of time or not, all that matters after contact is treatment of the dis-ease. Without treatment, the heart becomes susceptible to being contaminated with poisons such as bitterness, grudges, depression, negativity, pessimism, narcissism, self-hatred, doubt, and more.

The hard part about the whole *"dirty hands"* thing is that detecting who is entering your life with the wrong intention isn't easy. Depending on whether or not you're tired of waiting for the right companion, friend, or opportunity, detective work is the last thing you want to do. Still, it seems that the only choice is to pay in the beginning with waiting for something bad to happen as a sign or pay even more in the end with heartbreak unless you do the one thing that can help you avoid paying at all:

Ask God for the gift of discernment.

The gift of discernment is the supernatural ability to understand someone else's spiritual intent. People do what they do because their spirit is broken and if we get caught up on the front they're putting on, then we'll never see the truth. Ask God for the gift and He will give it to you, but until you can trust what you perceive through this gift, you must ask the Lord to keep the heart clear of infection.

Your goal today is to ask for a clean heart to be created within you and flush out infections like misery, resentment, regret, envy, shame, greed, jealousy, and anything else that entered your heart after someone broke it. Otherwise, you will change for the worse for good and become the one with *"dirty hands"* breaking hearts.

Praying Psalms 51:10 works two ways because it not only prevents you from becoming contaminated after being hurt, but it will heal you if contamination is running through your veins.

Say this prayer in faith:

"Father, create in me a clean heart. Help me to not allow the people who hurt me and the things I've had to face in life change me into someone You never meant for me to be. Keep me from becoming cold-hearted and stone-hearted and give me balance, wisdom, understanding, the ability to forgive, and insight to know when I should deny access to the secret places of my heart. Help me to not go after things that You didn't give me and never wanted for me. Search my heart and heal my wounds. Search my heart and be the Surgeon who removes each stone, especially

stones of unforgiveness. Then fill that space with Your Spirit. Search my heart and keep me covered in the areas where I am weak, for You are my Strength and Your healing love is my portion. I receive your answer Father.

In Jesus' name, Amen."

Day 30

♥

Psalms 73:26 My flesh and my heart faileth: but God is the strength of my heart, and my portion for ever.

There will be times when you won't have the strength to continue the path you started on, nonetheless have the courage to keep figuring out how to make it all work. Life, and the people in it, can fill your world with so many issues to resolve that they totally sap you of mental, emotional, and even physical strength. It's clear that when we do all and become all for some of everybody while running on empty, we are headed for a breakdown.

Our society and even our culture has trained us to think that we're strong based on how much we can take and how far we can go beyond the point of needing rest. The kudos are plenty when women keep going while broken, in pain, brutally hurt, devastated, and severely mistreated. Since so many people depend on us to ignore our own needs for the sake of theirs, too many of us are paying no mind to our hearts until the pain overwhelms us. It's usually not until we're forced that we give in and rest in the fact that everyone and everything will have to be just fine without us.

Question:

What if we arrived at that conclusion in peace instead of pieces?

The fact of the matter is that we need someone to be to us what we are to everyone else and if we are never weak and never in need of rest then we will never experience God's strength. It's only when we allow ourselves to be at peace with not being all and doing all for everybody that we get to know what it feels like to have Someone be our answer.

Since God is our portion forever, that means that we have what we need from Him now and in eternity. That also means that everyone pulling on you for a resolution also has what they need from Him now and in eternity. Excuse me when I say this, but you ain't always the answer Sis! As a matter of fact, you're in the way of your loved ones knowing God the way you do because of your fulfilling their every need.

Instead of being forced into balance through a breakdown, choose to lay down in His strength.

Day 29

♥

Philipians 4:7 And the peace of God, which passeth all understanding, shall keep your hearts and minds through Christ Jesus.

There is nothing like God's peace!

It reaches past our fears and pains into the depths of our souls.

Like a ray of sunshine, it warms us until it overpowers the frost from the cold and fright from the darkness.

The idea of God's peace can be hard to fathom when our experiences have made us feel like there will never be an end to the hurt and turmoil. Without an end in sight, we may be prone to making temporary decisions that have permanent results. To sum it up, the acts of making hasty decisions come from desperation and the presence of consequences from bad choices are clues that your emotions are leading you.

When your emotions lead you, your vision becomes blurry and your ability to make good decisions is impaired. Next thing you know, you've become so flustered that you've rearranged your plans and your life just to accommodate a temporary distraction. BUT, when the peace of God is leading you, you will always have your head on straight and your heart in-tact. When the peace of God is leading you, you can continue to direct the affairs of your life with excellent focus as you continue moving toward the goal(s).

As you go throughout your day and your coming days, think about the people, places, and things you hastily rearranged when you were desperate for an immediate answer to a temporary problem. Write down the common factors that pushed you to the point of desperation. Then ask God to heal you and help you receive His peace in times of fear and trouble.

Day 28

♥

Colossians 3:2 Set your affection on things above, not on things on the earth.

Disappointment comes when there's an expectation for one thing, but a different result is received. Missing out on the house, the car, the job, the trip, the shoes, the clothes, the friend, the relationship, and whatever else your heart desires can put us in a state of dismay all the way to depression. If you're there, or are on your way there, you need to reset your focus immediately!

When it comes to life, it's important to prioritize and be thankful for what we call *"the little things"*, which are really major! Things like walking, talking, making a fist, or the ability to comb our own hair are often overlooked because it comes so easy to us. We tend to take these things and only give our undivided thanks when they're absent.

In the same manner, we take those little yet major abilities for granted, we do so spiritually. Things like the ability to have an answer from Heaven manifest in the earth through prayer and declaration, the assistance of Angels, and the love of The Father will always outweigh what you missed out on any day. Now, I'm one for setting goals, but I'm also aware that we can't solely focus our soul's desire on them. If we do, we will die off when they die off!

When we set our affection on things above first and foremost, we are never disappointed because what's above is not only guaranteed, but it's better than what we had in mind in the first place.

You will never top what God has in store for you!

Let me say that again, you will never top what God has in store for you!

The best way to move past the disappointment over what you wanted but didn't get is to focus on what God has already blessed, not the mess!

Day 27

♥

Isaiah 26:3 Thou wilt keep him in perfect peace, whose mind is stayed on thee: because he trusteth in thee.

It's hard to keep focus when everyone and everything is trying to get your attention. You may only see it as everyone wanting a piece of your wisdom, guidance, and advice because you're naturally good at it, but as you probably guessed it gets deeper!

See, your attention is valuable and whoever or whatever holds it, owns you. You don't always know it at first, but when you give your undivided attention there's an exchange that takes place. If you're careless about entertaining the wrong thing, or even the right thing at the wrong time, your priorities go on pause. If left on pause for too long, you might end up trading your dreams, your goals, your readiness for opportunities, your peace, and your happiness for failure and missed opportunities. A looming sense of failure can lead to stress, anxiety, depression, and even resentment for life itself!

When we hear about having a need for the peace of God, we instantly think of ourselves being the ones going through a hard time. We never really stop to think that having a need for the peace of God may revolve around the fact that we've placed more than we can handle on our plate.

While it's important to know that God will restore your peace if you lose it, it's also important to keep the peace He gave you in the first place!

Why continue to ask The Father for the same thing because you keep losing it? I mean, you can keep asking, but all I'm saying is don't waste the answer when you get it! The next time your attention is summoned, evaluate what you'll have to give up in place of your priorities and if the peace God gave you must be exchanged for someone else's problem, don't make it your problem.

Some jobs are a job for you and other jobs are a job for Jesus!

Know the difference!

Day 26

♥

Matthew 5:8 Blessed are the pure in heart: for they shall see God.

You will see God in your state of mind.

You will see God in your speech.

You will see God in your character.

You will see God in your creativity.

You will see God in your love life.

You will see God in your family.

You will see God in your ministry.

You will see God on your job.

You will see God in your business.

You will see God in your education.

You will see God in the boardroom.

You will see God at the table to close the deal.

You will see God as a Healer.

You will see God as a Protector.

You will see God as a Provider.

You will see God as Father.

You will see God as Redeemer.

You will see God as Comforter.

Whatever area of your life is broken becomes a sign that you will see God!

Cry it out, scream it out, walk it out, write it out, sing it out, pray it out, but whatever you do, don't let what happened to you stop you from keeping your heart pure.

If you do, you stop yourself from seeing God's next move in the area you need it most.

Stay pure in your heart Sis, stay pure!

Day 25

♥

Matthew 11:29 Take my yoke upon you, and learn of me; for I am meek and lowly in heart: and ye shall find rest unto your souls.
30 For my yoke is easy, and my burden is light.

The cares of life will try to yoke you up and choke you out.

The cares of this world will feel heavy on the neck and if you have more than one care, it's no longer a necklace, it's a shackle.

Can you imagine every heartache, every bill, every man, woman, and child that you care about, every unfulfilled dream, and anything else you're concerned about hanging around your neck and resting on your shoulders?

Can you imagine having nobody to help you carry the weight?

Now, while I agree that what doesn't kill you

will only make you stronger, I also believe that wearing that kind of *"jewelry"* only teaches you to bend under pressure. That weight teaches you how to bow to the weight of the world on your head and shoulders.

To add insult to injury, you must be careful of people who only want to help you now so they can hurt you later.

There's so much to consider and all I can tell you is that Jesus is not like any of them. As a matter of fact, He lived, died, and is risen so that you would give your weight in exchange for His weight. His weight, His yoke, is light because He helps you to balance the assignments you were made for. That balance requires you to take off anything you're not supposed to carry and allow your strength to be used for what matters to Him.

What's on your plate Sis? Is it training you to bow?

Look at it all and give it God.

How do you do that? You pray KNOWING that the Lord heard you ahead of time, has answered you ahead of time, then go live in the freedom to be free!

Day 24

♥

Luke 12:34 For where your treasure is, there will your heart be also.

One of two things is happening with those tormenting memories:

1. What happened is constantly replaying in your mind.
2. You haven't processed what happened and don't plan on it.

I'm all for remembering what happened to know the strength of your overcoming ability, but what I'm not for is being stuck on the same scene!

Whatever happened to you wasn't fair, it wasn't right, and was downright cruel, but if you let the situation take space in your mind, the dust of it will fill your heart.

What thoughts and feelings are you collecting

in that mind and heart of yours?

Whatever they are, how do you erase what's taking space in your place?

The answer is, you have to make some new memories under one condition: *Focus on the details along the way, not the end goal of having a new memory.*

Think about it, the reason why it's hard to erase certain memories is because of the emotions associated with them. Learn to enjoy the details along the way to making a new memory and you'll have a new focus with new emotions attached.

Your focus always determines the state of your heart and where your mind is *(that's your treasure Sis)*, your heart is there also.

Day 23

♥

Psalm 119:11-12 Thy word have I hid in mine heart,
that I might not sin against thee.

Sin is knowing God's way of doing things and then doing those things your way anyway. These days we hear *"when you know better you do better"* and even when we know God's word, doing things His way isn't always easy.

God's way can put you out there on a limb.

God's way can have you be the one to make peace when you never made the mess in the first place.

God's way can have people thinking you're naive and gullible when you're really two seconds away from SHUTTING. IT. DOWN.

BUT! There's a flip side to God's way.

If you go out on a limb following God, it won't break.

If you make peace where you didn't make war, you'll receive the royal benefits that come from being a child of The King.

If you prefer what God says about you over the what people say about you, those same people will eat their words for the rest of your blessed life. Although the goal is not necessarily payback, it sure does feel good when God shuts the mouths of naysayers!

I have to ask you, what are you doing your way instead of God's way and how is that working out for you so far?

Take a moment to answer the question for your own knowledge. When you've answered the question, go back into prayer and ask for help to get back on track to the will of God.

Then, don't just talk about it, be about it!

Day 22

♥

*1 Samuel 16:7 for man looketh on the outward appearance,
but the LORD looketh on the heart.*

I know everyone reading this book loves to feel confident by looking good, but for the one who values opinions of others, be careful not to let your confidence cross over to arrogance.

Making ourselves feel better by putting someone down with our looks is an indication that we have some uglies within. If you've ever found yourself feeling or thinking like what I've described in the last two paragraphs then more than likely, you've been judged by others and it stuck with you to the point that you've become like the ones you were judged by.

All that matters is what we look like when we

take it all off?

Take away the hair, the makeup, the clothes, the job, the car, the house, and anything else that helps boost confidence and what's left?

Are you kind, are you patient, are you honest, are you sincere?

Is your heart still available?

Because it's your heart being close to the heart of the Lord that gets you into Heaven, not your beauty nor opinions.

Day 21

♥

Genesis 24:42-46

42 And I came this day unto the well, and
said, O LORD God of my master Abraham, if
now thou do prosper my way which I go: 43
Behold, I stand by the well of water; and it
shall come to pass, that when the virgin cometh
forth to draw *water*, and I say to her, Give me,
I pray thee, a little water of thy pitcher to drink;
44 And she say to me, Both drink thou, and I
will also draw for thy camels: *let* the
same *be* the woman whom the LORD hath
appointed out for my master's son. 45 *And*
before I had done speaking in mine heart,
behold, Rebekah came forth with her pitcher
on her shoulder; and she went down unto the
well, and drew *water*: and I said unto her, Let
me drink, I pray thee. 46 And she made haste,

and let down her pitcher from her *shoulder*, and said, Drink, and I will give thy camels drink also: so I drank, and she made the camels drink also.

I have only 7 words for you today:

GOD HEARD YOU AND IT'S ALREADY DONE!

Day 20

♥

Deuteronomy 4:39 Know therefore this day, and consider it in thine heart, that the Lord he is God in heaven above, and upon the earth beneath: there is none else.

One thing about God, He will not be second place in your life! There are so many things that we put in front of God although He's made a way for us to have those things. Sometimes we don't realize that our relationship with God is a real, live companionship.

In any relationship, we can't have the number one spot in someone's heart and not return the gesture. For some people, God doesn't get the number one spot because they feel He left them out. You know how it goes! He didn't make it happen, or prevent it from happening, or make them change, etc. When God does not fulfill our expectations, we are disappointed and sometimes it's heartbreaking to believe that He didn't come through for us.

The truth is that we have to align our expectations with His desires because it does not work the other way around. You see, even if God never does what you expect Him to, He has done so much for you already. If you don't agree with that then how about this:

He is God all by Himself, He never needed your help, and He's only asked you for your heart over and above anything else you have to offer.

Think about it! God, The Creator of the Milky Way, the planets, the sun, the moon, the stars, the flowers, trees, oxygen, and mankind is the same One who knows the exact number of hairs on your head. He is the same One who chooses to bottle up every tear you've ever cried and save it. He is the same One who sees you for who you are and still loves you as if you've never disappointed Him.

On a side note, you and I both know that if God was a man out here in these streets, we'd be 100% faithful! No questions asked!

Nobody and nothing deserves His spot and if you feel like God does not do enough for you, He's still God and deserves your respect!

At all times, give God what you owe Him.

Give Him the number one slot in your heart.

Day 19

♥

Proverbs 2:2 So that thou incline thine ear unto wisdom,

and apply thine heart to understanding;

It takes guts to try and understand where someone, especially the one who hurt you, is coming from. Now, I'm not talking about hearing out someone who wants to use their moment with you to manipulate you. Instead, I'm talking about having a moment where you raise your level of maturity to understand someone else's heart instead of yours only.

It takes a special heart and mind to think about someone else's point of view and hear them out without plotting a clapback in advance. When you do that, you are giving them a moment to be understood and in turn, you get to understand why he or she did what they did.

So how does understanding why someone hurt you benefit you?

A deeper look helps take the sting out of the offense. A conversation will always bring out the reasons why they are who they are and did what they did. Your job is to make room for understanding the root of his/her issue more than your fury and your point!

Disclaimer: This ain't for everybody! A heart to heart only works for people who are willing to be open and honest. Use this option carefully and wisely.

Day 18

♥

Proverbs 2:10-11 When wisdom entereth into thine heart, and knowledge is pleasant unto thy soul; 11 Discretion shall preserve thee, understanding shall keep thee:

It's easy to detect when someone doesn't like you.

They may give you a certain look, have a particular body language every time you come around, and may even change their tone should they have to speak to you. When people show their negative thoughts and feelings for you on their sleeve, appreciate them because they've made your job easy! The hardest part of your job is knowing who has the right motive.

Seeing past someone's words requires a different skill and your arsenal is incomplete without wisdom.

Wisdom changes the entire game for you! Wisdom helps you to know the truth about people in ways you never thought possible. Wisdom helps you determine your next move regarding your connection to a person, place, or thing. Wisdom helps you figure out if what you see in a person is just a flaw or if they're unwilling to change for the better. When you ask for Wisdom, you'll never be led by your emotions and the information that wisdom provides you will protect you.

Protect you from what? From giving your time, energy, support, money, and heart to someone or something that will only use you or waste you. After all the chances you've given to people, places, and things, you owe it to yourself to let wisdom take the lead!

Day 17

♥

Proverbs 3:5-6 Trust in the Lord with all thine heart; and lean not unto thine own understanding. 6 In all thy ways acknowledge him, and he shall direct thy paths.

Simply put, we women run things!

We run the house, our position at the job, the business, the ministry, the charity, the bills, the school, and so much more! We're so good at it that we forget that we don't run us!

Since we're constantly making decisions for everyone and everything else, we usually make decisions for our life without consulting God. If we're not consulting God, we are running ourselves into the ground. How can it be that you have everything and everyone on the right track except you?

This is where we get ourselves into trouble!

Just because we are doing good things, does not mean that we're doing what God wants us to do. It's essential that we invite Him into our life and make Him our Leading Partner by asking for His help and waiting for His answer. When we do, we run us too and finally have all things on point and fully balanced.

Day 16

♥

Proverbs 4:23 Keep thy heart with all diligence; for out of it are the issues of life.

In the same way precious jewels are guarded in a museum is the same way you must guard your heart.

You must keep it centered under the spotlight in the room, set a certain temperature for the right atmosphere, set up a beautiful display that allows gems to be seen but not touched carelessly, surround it in a glass that's hard to break, and be on guard for thieves, vandals, and people who underestimate your value.

You must be careful to only allow your heart to be taken out of the glass when someone has permission from God. Do you think anyone can walk up to a priceless gem in a museum and just touch it? Nope! If touching is allowed, they have to receive permission first or else touching becomes a violation and that's cause for removal.

Your heart is just like a gem; act like it!

Day 15

♥

Proverbs 13:12 Heaviness in the heart of man maketh it stoop:
but a good word maketh it glad.

You are just one word away from a better relationship with the Lord.

You are just one word away from a good day.

You are just one word away from happiness and joy.

You are just one word away from peace.

You are just one word away from restoration.

You are just one word away from healing.

You are just one word away from prosperity.

You are just one word away from newness.

You are just one word away from a second chance.

You are just one word away from opportunity.

You are just one word away from forgiveness.

You are just one word away from salvation.

You are just one word away from entrepreneurship.

You are just one word away from that degree.

You are just one word away from the house.

You are just one word away from the life God called you to live and that word is *"Yes"* to God.

That word is going to cost you something, but you're already paying the price of your *"No"* and it's a price that your heart can no longer afford to pay!

Day 14

Proverbs 13:12 Hope deferred maketh the heart sick: but when the desire cometh, it is a tree of life.

When family becomes unfamiliar, and friends become unfriendly, and when a lover becomes unloving, it starts to feel like you can't depend on anyone to keep their promise to you.

Somehow, the experiences we have with people creep into our perception of The Father and when He refuses to move past His timing, it can seem like He is just like everyone else.

The truth is that waiting is heavy! We wait on relatives to come through, wait on aces to come through, and wait on companions to come through too, and when they can't that's usually the time we finally decide to wait on God.

I want you to know that God's focus is on the end game. The end game is that you not only obtain the blessings, but that you maintain the blessings! The deal is that you can't hold onto the blessing long term if you arrive at the blessing short processed.

With that said, there will be times when you feel like *"it's"* never going to happen. It will hurt and the weight of the wait will be heavy, but when the process is over and the promise manifests, you'll be all you need to be in order to maintain all you've gained.

Day 13

♥

Proverbs 17:22 A merry heart doeth good like a medicine:
but a broken spirit drieth the bones.

Waking up on the right side of the bed is effortless. Maybe it was a good night's rest or that you had a good night overall, but either way waking up on the right side of the bed isn't something that we plan.

Waking up on the wrong side of the bed isn't as effortless. Maybe you cried yourself to sleep, maybe you had a lonely night, or maybe you feel you have nothing to look forward to. When you wake up after a bad night, it's clear why you woke up on the wrong side of the bed.

I've been there and all I can tell you is to go and get some medicine! Medicine in this instance is not a drink, a drug, a man, or any other substance. Treat your heartache like a real wound and how do we heal a wound? We let it breathe!

Although we can't see heartache, you can bring air to your heart by doing something new along with doing some healthy things you haven't done in a while. Always be sure to air out your entire thoughts and feelings in prayer too! Then get up, get out, and get something knowing, believing, and trusting that God heard it all, saw it all, and has already provided the healing you need.

Day 12

Proverbs 23:17 Let not thine heart envy sinners: but be thou in the fear of the Lord all the day long

They didn't get away with anything!

You may not see it now and for some, you may not be allowed to see it now, but trust that God is on the case! The best part about it is that you don't have to say a word.

I have to tell you, not saying a word isn't for the weak. You will be viewed as a coward when you remain silent after being mistreated or humiliated. You may even feel like a coward, but your truth is that you heard God, you know God, and you're being obedient in letting Him speak for you! That's the difference between how you handle things and how everyone else handles things. You know that God is not a liar and whatsoever a man sows, he reaps. Nobody is going to get in the way of you sowing good seeds for a bountiful harvest at all times!

Now here's the trick, these same people who did you wrong will be blessed too and when you see this, it makes you wonder if you should start moving the way your enemies move.

Can I share something with you?

Sometimes people have to get really high before they get knocked down low, but above all else, it's God's prerogative to rain and shine on the just and the unjust. His blessings are still His business so don't touch that with a ten-foot pole!

Stay up Sis! They are not getting over and when it's time for them to learn their lesson, they'll be looking at you with the Lord behind your back because that's exactly where He's got you!

He's got your back!

Day 11

♥

Proverbs 14:30 A sound heart is the life of the flesh:
but envy the rottenness of the bones.

Simply put, a healing heart can save your life, but jealousy will eat you alive.

Healing is going to cost you something! There may be times when you'll have to cry alone, be misunderstood, have some restless nights, lose your appetite, and even lose some people, but as long as you're healing, you're on the right track!

Healing also shows you your reflection! It's going to make you take a good look at what happened and it won't leave your part in things out of the picture. The healing process shows you why you trusted that kind of person in the first place, what issues you haven't dealt with, where your faith is, and even where your self-esteem is.

After your self-evaluation, the healing process will move you to action. You may have to do things that make you uncomfortable like talking to yourself as gently as you would someone else's child, speaking blessings out loud, forgiving yourself, remaining quiet, examining your motives, and even speaking up for yourself.

What's your price for healing and are you really ready to pay for it?

Day 10

♥

Proverbs 15:28 The heart of the righteous studieth to answer:

but the mouth of the wicked poureth out evil things.

There's danger in having a fit of rage in public!

Society has replaced Paparazzi and anyone having a fit of rage can become a celebrity.

When people explode, they're liable to spew curses and I'm not talking about profanity!

The curses I'm referring to are foul phrases like, you ain't *s&%#*, you're a piece of *s(^%*, that's why you don't have nothing, you ain't worth a damn, and so many other phrases that are directly opposite of what God said about us.

Each time someone allows their words to be based on a hot temper, they bring the wrong things to life!

I say pick and choose your battles as best you can, but when you feel that rage coming upon your tongue, be quiet until you can speak your truth in peace!

The reason is that you don't want to have any record, digitally or spiritually, of being the one who cursed someone's life. The viral videos of people losing their cool is a proof of instant reaping too. They're spewing curses on someone else, but the effects of humiliation are coming right back on them with the push of a button.

Always make it a practice to think before you speak!

Day 9

♥

Proverbs 17:22 A merry heart doeth good like a medicine:

but a broken spirit drieth the bones.

You may not have had the choice in preventing your heart from being broken, but the decision to move on is all yours!

First, you have to acknowledge what's wrong, then identify where that feeling is coming from, and finally take what's needed to help restore your heart back to it's normal function.

Your choice of spiritual medicine is totally different from the meds we take for our physical body. Heart medicine is gratefulness, joy, peace, love, forgiveness, and other spiritual doses that you don't see, but can feel! Take any of those meds and you'll find that your heart will be better than it was before, but if you choose to stay broken your strength won't return.

Don't stay paralyzed between two choices because of what happened to you. Choose to have a merry heart over bitterness, sadness, despair, complaints, anger, and anything that dries your life.

Day 8

♥

Proverbs 18:12 Before destruction the heart of man is haughty,

and before honour is humility.

Sis, you can't go high unless you go low.

I'm not talking about cutting people down, gossiping, setting people up, or anything like that. What I'm talking about is how you think of yourself compared to how you think of God!

A lot of times, we do things without God because we didn't think to ask Him for instruction. We bring the big things to Him, but we have a tendency to overlook His direction in our everyday lives. I'm sure He doesn't mind which supermarket or furniture store you choose to visit, but what if He has a special blessing for you at His store of choice? It's possible that God doesn't mind which road you take home, but what if He wants to spare you from traffic so that you have more time to do what you're called to do?

The point is that just because you feel you can do what you want, doesn't mean you should do it without Him. Furthermore, doing life without asking God is the biggest sign of haughtiness because we're choosing our ideas over His will.

Instead, we have to make our own opinions bow down to the will of God by being mindful to invite Him into everything.

Your way is not higher than God's way.

Your thoughts are not higher than His thoughts and when you acknowledge Him in all things, He can trust you with anything!

Lay down your will to take up His will and you can only rise!

Day 7

Proverbs 21:2 Every way of a man is right in his own eyes:
but the Lord pondereth the hearts.

You know why we women have a hard time being wrong?

It's because we're always right! LOL!

Okay, okay, we're not always right, but we have a great average when it comes to hitting the nail on the head! Since there have been so many times when what we said would happen happened, it's hard for us to admit our mistakes and admit when we're wrong.

Admitting our flaws makes us vulnerable and the fact is, it's hard to be vulnerable and wrong at the same time! The thought behind this idea is *what will the people in my world think of me when they find out that I was wrong?*

Admitting you're wrong says that you're risking being seen with flaws that may cause others to reject you and rejection is hard!

You're going to have to take a chance on the ones you love. They may reject you, they may not, but either way you are capable of being strong enough to be vulnerable in front of others.

It's okay to say I'm sorry. It's okay to admit that you're wrong.

It's okay to be vulnerable.

Lastly, where you were rejected, God has fully and openly received you! Remember that more than anything else.

Day 6

♥

Proverbs 23:7 For as he thinketh in his heart, so is he

We have over 70,000 thoughts a day and it's hard to catch them all, inspect them, and decide what goes or stays. Most thoughts are involuntary, but what about the voluntary thoughts in your mind? What about the thoughts you think on purpose?

Your intentional thoughts are most important because your belief in them brings those thoughts to life. In other words, if you think you're capable, you're capable. If you think you can't, then you never will.

Thinking must be on purpose! The hard part of intentional thinking is remembering to do what you believe in the face of a hard time in life. As a matter of fact, the thing we usually say when we're in the middle of a hard place is, "I can't even think straight". In these cases, it's hard to come out from underneath the rock that landed on you! Instead of just laying there, you have to prepare yourself with an affirmation that you can believe in at all times and at all costs.

In the space below, I challenge you to create an affirmation statement that works for you. Write an affirmation that you can imagine thinking and saying through the tears. Once you're finished, memorize your words and speak them out loud every day a few times a day.

By the time that rock tries to use you for a landing pad, you'll be standing on top of it rather than it standing on top of you!

If you're doing it right, you should be writing your affirmation over and over until it encompasses who you are in life!

Book of Tasha

The last 5 days are based on the wisdom God has blessed me with at my lowest lows and my highest highs.

I've found that when we're in a dark place for a long time, any bit of light that comes our way makes us believe the dark times are gone for good.

On the flip side, a prolonged dark experience can also prevent us from basking in the sunlight because we believe that only a bad time is just around the corner.

The truth is that darkness and light are part of life, but I want to challenge you to see the contrast between the two from my perspective. I believe that we are all full of life and our life is filled with light at all times. Whenever darkness shows up, it's trying to make us believe that we aren't full of life and that our life is only filled with darkness. Could it be that darkness rears it's ugly head when you know the truth and are living in truth? Could it be that darkness is simply a pop quiz to see if you remember the foundational truths you stand on? The thing is, there's no pop quiz if you don't show up for class and if you don't show up for class, then you won't graduate, and if you don't graduate, then you won't be certified to teach anyone else! You must keep showing up through the good and the bad! These nuggets I'm about to share with you have helped me in the middle of my storms as well as helped me bask in the sunshine.

Read one each day and when you finally arrive at Day 1, write your own devotional and let it be your new beginning.

Day 5

♥

Tasha 1:1 - You can prevent a broken heart with a focused mind.

It's going to be very easy to guard your heart when you work on maintaining your mindset. See, most people think things like *"don't get too close too soon", "don't fall in love too quick", "don't give so much in the beginning".* Those ideas all relate to the heart, but the truth is, you'll never do the most too fast or too soon when your mindset is intact.

Whenever you're entertaining something or someone new, set your mind on celebrating what the experience is doing for you, what the experience is teaching you about you, and what the experience is adding to your life.

When you're focused on the lessons first, it's hard to be disappointed when things don't work out the way the heart wanted.

Day 4

*Tásha 1:2 - If you never hit the goal,
you'll hit many and plenty along the way!*

Baby, reach for the stars!

Baby, be unrealistic!

Baby, go for something that's beyond what you've seen and what you know!

It's your right and duty to set high goals way beyond your reach and it's okay to never feel guilty about having high standards or feel bad about not reaching them.

Here's why: When you reach for the stars from the ground you're standing on, the journey alone is going to take you further than you've ever been!

You'll get to see the ground look like a patch of grass.

You'll get to see treetops look like heads of broccoli.

All of a sudden, the wind that used to take your breath away is now the wind beneath your wings helping you soar. You'll get to see your side of the world as just a piece fitting into the planet and not the whole world.

High standards and far out goals can balance your perspective on your life. As you continue to elevate, what seemed too big, too much, or too hard is now believed to be easy and possibly unimportant.

The point is, if you never come face to face with the stars you were aiming for, let alone be able to put your hand on them, there will be some clouds you've touched along the way in your starry quest. That's still more than you've ever had and more than you've ever done!

Day 3

Tasha 1:3 – Up is down, in is out, over is under.

If you're ever going to reach the next level, it's not going to be through arrogance.

Most times, when a promotion or upgrade is at your door, there's usually someone begging you to disrespect them. They're literally asking for *"it"* and by *"it"* I mean, they want you to cuss them out! They want you to floss and show them who's boss! They must want the hands based on the way they keep talking to you, and sleeping on you, and acting toward you right? Right!…but you and I both know the real answer is "wrong"!

Provokers will always be part of life and if you give into their tactics, you will have to repeat the course of your lesson. It's important to evaluate whether or not you're going to let the satisfying feeling of checking someone lead you or if you're going to let love lead.

Your next-level-life is always going to appear with a final test in the area of your humility. When you refrain from doing what you KNOW will destroy a person's ego or refrain from proving your point, you're truly ready for the upgrade!

Day 2

♥

Tasha 1:4 – Do it scared Sis.

There will always be a reason why you shouldn't remain focused, why you shouldn't shoot for the stars, why you shouldn't remain humble, and all of these reasons stem from fear. I know it doesn't seem that deep, but when you process your thoughts and emotions down to the motive, it only gets deeper!

When it comes to remaining focused, most people will find a distraction to blame in fear of giving their all for nothing. When it comes to shooting for the stars, people aim low in fear of coming back empty handed. When it comes to remaining humble, people prove their point in fear of being mistaken for someone they're not. Everything won't always work out on your watch Sis. You will set out to do big things and sometimes the results turn up little to nonexistent and that's okay!

Big thangs ain't easy and you might have to strike out a few times before you hit a home-run. I know there are people watching who have too much to say, but Sis, the only one with enough courage to swing is you!

Day 1

♥

Tasha 1:5 - Your heart, your life, your happiness, your success is your responsibility.

I know there are so many people and things that can get in the way of what I shared with you in the last chapter. You may run into some miserable days and for some of you reading this book, you're still suffering from the moment trouble ran into you. I get it. I understand it, but hear my heart through this page when I say:

THAT'S NOT THE END FOR YOU.

We hear it so often, *"you're not what happened to you"*, and it's true, but only if you make it a reality in your life. You're not a victim, but you will be if you refrain from living life because of what happened to you. You gotta flip it! For example, if the man who hurt you had a beard, it doesn't mean stay away from men with beards. If the friend who hurt you had blonde hair, it doesn't mean to never befriend a blonde again. It's important to take a moment and evaluate why you're making the decisions you're making. Ask yourself why do I want this, why don't I want this, where did this desire or lack thereof come from, and keep asking questions until you arrive at the root.

If the root is grounded in who you are at your core, go for it, but if the root is solely based on your pain, you still need to go for it!

Hurt and disappointment comes in all shapes and sizes, but joy and success does too; remember that!

Made in the USA
Middletown, DE
18 February 2023